slitting the tongues of jackdaws

Eilish Martin

Eilish Martin

Happy Christmas Sean +
Merry New Year,
take care
Roisin
& Michael

SUMMER PALACE PRESS

First published in 1999 by

Summer Palace Press
Cladnageeragh, Kilbeg, Kilcar, County Donegal, Ireland

© Eilish Martin, 1999

Printed by Nicholson & Bass Ltd.

A catalogue record for this book is available
from the British Library

ISBN 0 9535912 1 2

for
my mother and father

Acknowledgments

Some of the poems in this book have previously appeared in:

HU; New Irish Writing, Sunday Tribune (1995); *Omnibus* (Belfast 1997); *Word of Mouth* (Belfast 1996) and *Women's Works* (Wexford 1995, 1996, 1997, 1998).

Some poems have also been broadcast by BBC Radio Ulster, BBC N.I. TV and RTE.

Biographical Note
Eilish Martin was born in Belfast in 1945. After graduating from Trinity College Dublin she became a teacher of English and has taught in London and Belfast. She was short-listed for a Hennessy Award in 1995 and in the same year was a prize winner in the National Women's Poetry competition. She is a member of the Word of Mouth poetry collective.

CONTENTS

Of Earth and Air

Though you laboured in a shortened bed between narrow sheets,
biting on your tongue till it bled, I was born elsewhere.

My birthing pool can be found in the meltwater of a dream where you
briefly stood your ground,

your skirt caught on the yellow gorse, abandonded for a loose shift
of water, your feet bedded

on pebbles the colour of pewter, your arms a hoop of shadow
nursing my head in its lap.

And you, a curse under your breath, knotting the bright
thread you were already winding
back into your purse,

my upside-down screech, held by the heels, mocking
the howl of the north wind in the gorse
bloating your skirt.

A Death in Autumn

They probably caught her in a strange bed
and it being Samhain (the evidence suggests) their outrage led
to a ritual retribution. Naturally
there were procedures. That would have been fully
understood by every party concerned
including the victim, whose role in these affairs was just as learned
as that of prosecutor, judge and foreman of the jury.
Although, if truth be told, one masked actor usually played all three
and if he felt inclined to extemporise,
the mob (in the pit or in the gods) would be none the wiser,
believing the script was sealed
by the wand that marked her flesh for the common weal.

They have untied the knots of my apron strings,
unhooked my bodice, loosed my gathered skirt, pulled off my rings.
They have unpinned my curls, let fall my hair.
My head they have razored bare.

Yesterday I lay in a warm bed that was no trouble;
today I am naked, fallen, all a-stubble.
Yesterday plumped fingers reaped my flesh in celebration;
today I am poured out on fallow ground, a spilled libation.

I wonder (when all was said) did she put a brazen face on things,
shrugging off the taught disgrace of the noose that rings
her leathered neck with its unbroken promise
or did she tongue the wind, its breath hard against her lips.

Vocation

One minute he knew he was born
to walk on water, the next he was drowned – gone
under without leaving a stain.

There was nothing the other could do but turn back alone
into the deep field from where they had come,
his heart was already stretching towards home
and a door opening to be told of a drowned son.

Although he'll tell you how he fasted on water
and carried his brother shoulder high
above a late August afternoon for most of a year
blundering into honeycombs of bewildered sighs.

And his mother will say it was the drowned son
she saw coming home with quiet eyes, not making a sound,
his feet bone dry and barely touching the ground.

Waking

It is no time to wake her now
for she is rocking the baby to sleep
beside the fire
her head full of the lullaby
her arms heavy without their load
her heart nesting in the hawthorn.

It is no time to wake her now
for she is walking down the lane
between the brambles
her head full of the wind
her arms an empty shawl across her breast
her heart dropping out of its nest.

It is no time to wake her now
for she is digging a lazy-bed
behind the wall
her head full of the dream
her arms are laying down
her heart halved for setting in the ground.

It will be time enough to wake her
when she comes to the blackthorn
by nightfall. For she will be tired
with the rocking and the walking and the digging
and would sleep to wake in the dark
not able to find her way home.

4711

She wore *Eau de Cologne 4711*
like a PIN number.
Discreetly.

In her bottom drawer
french knickers and camisoles
picked up her scent while she slept.

Mother-of-pearl buttoned cuffs,
detachable lace collars left a trace
on the wrist, on the pulse below the ear.

Between finger and thumb
she held its negative
in a gloved hand.

Hemlines rumoured it
in the hollow
behind the knee.

In the vanity purse of her handbag
there was an empty bottle
without a stopper.

She taught me to wear all perfume that way
– on a garment's edge, on a tissue of lingerie,
on an empty hanger at the back of the wardrobe –
L'Aimant, Ecstasie, L'Enfant Perdue, Poison.
Memorised, then folded away.

Days of Abstinence

I have painted a woman bending over a sink,
running water through a collander of herring.
A woman who has sons and daughters.

Certain devices hint at intimacy

– her apron, an old shirt, its sleeves
wrapped around her waist
– a boning knife on the draining board, its handle
wound with cord for better grip.

And oh, the lustre of the woman's bare arms.

I have put a girl by this woman's side,
balancing on tiptoe, steadying herself against the sink

– a girl whose head is full of the figurine
on the mantelpiece in the front room, a porcelain
dancer with eyes fired to an all-over white
intent on the door, listening for her music
so she can begin.

But there, where the girl imagines the delph dancer, there
is where narrative steps outside its fixing agents
– the mediums of beeswax, of albumen,
of gum from the acacia tree –

leaving all kinds of plots to thicken in rooms
where everything,
even the utility furniture in chintz covers,
is waiting to begin,

and I become absorbed with the rust of blood
crusting under fingernails,
the brilliance of fishes' scales gloving a woman's hands,

the soluble quality of oil in ether

suggesting the robust grace
of two women roughed-in,
inclining towards one another
on days of abstinence.

Hawthorn and Rowan and Hazel

You will always be hawthorn to me
and rowan and hazel.

Hazel in your eyes
divining the damage
of hawthorn incense
in the house
plucked
out of the convent grounds
as the nuns sang
their Miserere.

I will always be lifting my finger
for you to see the thorn
lodged
under my skin
when I broke the branch.

You will always be letting fall
the hazel from your eyes
putting to one side
the broken hawthorn
wrapping your rowanberry red lips
around the wound
sucking
the thorn free.

A Mother Speaks

Now that it has come to pass
this is all I know,
I saw no star, there was no snow.
No shepherds came, no wise men.
No angels sang.
And though I'd carried my child low
the birth was slow. Slow.

And this I know.
Whilst our firstborn fed from my breast
my husband kindled a fire in the beasts' trough
and made an offering of the afterbirth.

Bruised

She wore a bruised strawberry
over her left breast.
I would never have guessed
if I hadn't seen her undress,
the summer I shared her bed,
the summer of grandfather's death.
She called it, *my allotment.*

Seeing my eyes linger
she explained it was given her
one summer in the plots,
by a man who smelled of mould and old tobacco.
Not that she had wanted more
than a lettuce, the root intact with soil,
to please her mother

              at home
stitching false hems by hand,
turning collars starting to fray;
and she had the coin to pay
in a purse hung
about her neck. But he took her
by surprise

with flowers;
the pink blue-flushed spike of lupin,
the foil of gypsophila's white veil
enticing her in to the mildew
grey of his shed
to show the secret tufted bed
where wild strawberries grow,
and.

When she turned to go
she slipped on some trodden thing
falling against the nail
that ripped her purse, spilling
its coppers on the earthen floor,
and tore the flesh above her breast,
that healed in its chastened way
to resemble a bruised strawberry
clotting close to her heart.

All that summer I lay
in the heat of her widow's bed
wide-eyed while she slept,
looking at the bruised fruit
she wore pinned to her breast,
unsure of how to say
I would wear it for her
when she was dead.

Kiloshine

*...............they lifted the two small bodies locked in death and
not being able to tell if they had been baptised, buried them at
Kiloshine in the ruins of the old church where the ghost of a
tall woman walks from time to time when the moon is full.*

In this place where the bones of one child rock
the bones of another in a limestone
hollow, the moon dreams me
in its pod of honesty,
its lumps of blank
seed, its husk.

Undone to the waist I bare the white scar
tissue of a breast to the hungry mouths
of children in the strip of ground
between two fields of winter
barley, the juice of young
nettles on my tongue.

No saint's mother, I could no more save you
from untimely death than save myself.
But rock me, rock me in your limestone
cot and suckle at my ruined breast
till wondrous holy water breaks
into unconsecrated ground.

Encounter

Each month, drawn by the silver of the new moon's lure,
I clamber over bare stones to the hermit's cell
to tuck up the skirts of my frock,
to rock myself in a stone cradle for the cure.
While below, in the limbs of a dead tree,
the scolding song of the storm cock
mocks and no cure comes to me.

Between heart and womb I am harr-hung,
lugged in the heart's eye, earthed in the womb's spud stone,
spanning the wind with hammered iron.
Shadows lean into me bending my rungs
to a slate grey flight making for home.

Still my rose-stipple trout thrashes
in a well of brash water
and the cursing stone
eclipses my bone.

No speckled pebble on the wing
tumbles my bright shilling out of the air.

I will catch snow in the space between my rungs,
feel the notch of frost, the slow graining of rain,
the sun's bind in bramble and woodbine.
I will grow old and be alone.

Still

it was then I climbed to the source of the Finny above
Lough Nafooey and dangling my legs over

the lip of a humpback bridge braced my feet against
a cushion of mountainy air

and waited for still waters to break into a burn
carrying seeds

of wild thyme under a babbling tongue
to a western sea.

Miscarriages

By saying, *Don't waste good breath cursing the dark*, he meant
the two of us should be consoled, less
baffled, reconciled anew with disappointment,

that foreknowing miscarriage we should be content with the given
sense of something longed for, withheld
– like biddable children, when they think of it, might think of heaven.

Until he heard the legend of a man night-fishing, who mistook his sure
footedness in the dark and overbalanced into Coire na mBan
to be delivered up testifying that a merry dance of brilliants lured

him to within a whisker of its undreamt source. And bursting
he re-emerged into the night, gasping for breath,
bewildered, inconsolably raging at the stars, given to cursing.

Second Sight

The way I heard it a man who'd lost his sight came to the island
having been told of the well's reputation
for healing and was taken by one of the islanders to a turning
in the road and pointed roughly in the well's direction.

An age passed before he ventured his right foot
and was all but confounded by the ground's determination
rushing upwards to support his first step
in just the right proportion

of shape to depth. Left foot followed right, each step
gaining on the shine earlier pilgrims
had put on the stones, till he felt buoyed and believed
he heard voices up ahead calling him

by his first name. Then he dared to imagine all living souls
on the island, having learned
about him from the guide, had left aside their work
and come to safeguard his journey,

when really he had just misheard an idle breeze worrying
the well's overarching thorns, and rounding
on himself at the cliff's edge his ears lit up at the inrushing
thunder of the tide running a mute moon to ground.

Aftermath

One of my slowest girls sits with her back to the wall
cutting out rough tongues of fire, pairs of ill-
matching wings from squares
of yellow sugar paper.

I watch in silence as she forms the letters
of the word *peace* in bright red felt-
tip on her limp tongues and wings,
then balance myself on the rung

of a stepladder, tying up her idea of the Holy
Ghost and a host of angels to every
fluorescent light fitting in the room
and climb back down, taking in the vroom

vroom presence of sulphur and brimstone
filling the whole room, the water-based vermilion
stiffening, with its mix of quicksilver, the resolve of wings
and tongues ascending and descending on varying lengths of string.

Flaw

The door into the street banged behind him
leaving the house shaking.

She picked up her knitting and paid out a string of wool
from the coiled skein, reining in the slack
at the knitting end where the clack
of needles recited the Aran pattern in gossipy rhythms,
the scheming needles idling away the waiting
till he returned.

Cable-twists, blackberry-knots, moss-weaves
spoke about an island race of fishermen
pitched in curraghs
against switchback breakers,
hauling fish from generation to generation.
And their women walking the shore,
tide tugging surf-shackled feet,
eyes skinned for boats black-
nippling the swell, ripe blobs of bramble fruit,
praying their incantations might pull the boats in
on rosary cords before the sea
would pluck and net them in tangle-weed.

A weave of women on moss, thirsting
lips brine-washed, slaked
by the letting of blackberry
stained tongues honing over dead men's bones.

She counted out the stitches she knew by rote
noting the Aran women made a flaw
so that fleshed bones redressed by salt
could be claimed by recognising the fault.

Then he was there, his face as off-white
as the unwashed wool cradled in her lap,
as oily, with the swelt of tears greasing his cheeks,

my friend is dead, my friend is dead, my friend is dead,

the one phrase repeating and repeating
as if the rhythm made the words less hard to say.

As if the rhythm made the words less hard to say.

Time Share

At 30,000 feet and climbing, approaching a speed of 560 miles an hour
we left Irish airspace behind.
Out of the blue

my youngest son, nine-and-a-half years old, said
not counting you and Dad and me being born
my best thing is the ceasefire

then pulling a face and plugging his ears he tuned in to the inflight movie,
leaving me strapped in, listening for the sound
of ice forming on a wing.

On the first night of our package holiday I walked on the edge
of the Mediterranean wearing nothing
but silver nymphs in my ears

and a Monsoon sarong double knotted
over my breast, its batik brushing
against my waxed bikini line.

The sea broke over my feet, washing what sounded like *Ulysses,*
Ulysses, onto the sand, pulling it back out
between my painted toenails

reminding me of Penelope, her heart as slack as an unstrung
bow, walking on the shore at Ithaca for twenty odd years,
the Aegean weaving between her toes

unravelling her prints in the sand. And Ulysses, after the sack of Troy,
safe in bed with a witch – thanks to the black root of wild rue,
a gift from the gods for his heart –

leaving behind on her king size sheets some of the blood on his hands
before going home to his wife and son wearing nothing
next to his skin but a suit of rags.

The Last Resort

My neighbour pours cream into a cracked saucer for her cat,
Moonshine, then comes to the wrought iron gate
between our gardens to tell me about the daughter
she calls her wayward girl, backpacking round the world,

behind her back Moonshine laps up the cream,

and how she's lost the cutting of sweet bay
I'd given her, because of unforgiving frosts in May.
I should never have left it so exposed.

I raise my hand as if attempting absolution,
wanting to say something about unaccountable Acts of God,
but she's already turned away to dead-head
her Boule de Neige, the old rose she grows
in a specially dug bed.

Last time she wrote she'd got as far as The Last Resort,
a regular stop-over, for those like her, on the road to Paradise.

Moonshine has licked the cracked saucer clean.

I've been letting my garden go;
its firethorn, ragged with woodbine,
its out-of-hand witch hazel, are close to wild.

I go there when I need to believe in prayer,
kneeling as if to trim the unkempt blue of forget-me-not,
pleading with some anonymous patron saint of all the wayward,
wherever they happen to be keep them safe from acts of god.

Paradise Fatigue

Above the falling blade of the Hatchet Field a cloud shrouds, a star
hums, a moon pendulums, a merlin scythes the air
with angled wings, a wind sings in the cat's cradle
of a transmission aerial.

Below Black Mountain a kneeling cherub with a fractured wing
swings from the jib of a crank and ratchet crane
in a monumental sculptor's yard strewn
with half-engraved memorials.

Under the sign of two beaten angels hanging by a brazen wing
at the place where six roads cross
a stolen zephyr brakes, spilling
strings of angel dust.

Elsewhere the wings of a broadsheet fold round the globe of a hazard
lamp alternating in circuits of blips and quarks
a quirk of light in the spaces
between the words.

Remission

To tell the story at all you must husband
words as dutifully as you husband
all worldly goods.

I make a space, picking through the grapes, thinning out
the bunches of fruit that will otherwise
succumb to mildew.

In the end you break the unbearable
silence, your words rushing
the glass roof.

Having out-lived the killing
the women had to think
about disease

– the lesions
refusing
to heal.

I made decisions,
this woman
would live

this other
die.

The ones who lived
made their own
way home,

the others we buried, one
in a sleeveless frock
I'd outgrown.

You say no more, preoccupied
– by the rain that has ruined
my ornamental poppies?

– by the rogue pain
in your amputated
breast?

If I could speak I'd speak
of stretching out beside you
in the wet grass

the both of us
awash with
rain

the orange petals
under our heads,

of keeping watch with you in sleep's tundra region
where dreams sink of themselves
into the permafrost

making manifest what is at chance - a woman
in a summer frock, drenched through and
through, crossing my threshold,

blessing herself, praying she can withstand the next fall
of snow

somewhere remote and equatorial.

Writing Back on All Saints' Day

We have no choice – around All Souls the ghosts of those
we write about possess us, insinuating themselves
into our space.

The dog you walk in a desolate place has more sense. For him a bird in a necklace
of thorns is fair game, he is familiar with feather and bone.
Failing the bird he'll root out her nest.

In the North, evacuated windows in an unwell house familiar with death
would oppress your tenacious ghost.

In my November orchard imagine her asleep. Her eyes would seem
the pulp of apples rotting down, an affliction of skins.

And wouldn't you know, our grey frontiers would leach the plush
of her velvet dress (the big red of haemorrhage) trailing
far horizons of land and sky, of sky and sea.

I drop through my own lines to where their temperature catches
my good wing and away I climb – remembering a derelict
instinct for home – a vagrant song thrush in each eye.

Airmail Letter

Here is my arm foreshortened
in its reach, picking up a friend's grief
between finger and thumb

wherever you are, empty
out your pockets

here is my hand with news of her son's death
ribboned with chevrons of flight
crumpled in a fist

— a stone for skimming across water
the fit of a closed hand

and my mouth snagged in the mirror
aghast at its old
phonetic pain

— a clasp knife for whittling bits of stick
the blade housed in its handle

my tongue's misgiving
crossing ahead of itself
into a life foreclosed

— a twist of salt in blue
tissue paper.

Epiphany in Bombay Street

He came from the east on a trolley bus
bringing him over the Queen's Bridge
from his digs in Empress Street,

a back attic room with a skylight that blurred
the stars where he plotted his journey
to Bombay Street on a threadbare map

by the light of a 40watt bulb, tracing its route till it came to an end
behind the Redemptorist Monastery, close to the Blue Star
taxi depot on the corner of the Kashmir Road.

He carried with him bars of Sunlight
and tins of Cherry Blossom
in a brown leather case

as crazed with laughter lines and crows' feet
as his face, arriving to the chiming
of *Sanctus, Sanctus, Sanctus,*

Benedictus qui venit in nomine Domini, running
his free hand along the monastery rails
as if turning a prayer wheel.

The women called him Raja-mataz and loved his oriental
eyes, his razzle-dazzle smile, his eastern promise,
the way he called them *lady*

and they bought his Sunlight and his Cherry Blossom crossing
his palm with coppers. His goods all gone he'd make time
to sit a while in Mrs. Devine's, smoking

turkish cigarettes, sipping Amber Glow from a china cup kept topped-up,
enjoying home-made cake spiced with caraway seed
while she drank mulled wine.

And for custom's sake, before returning to the east,
he'd call at the Midget Gem to buy Clove Rock,
Sugared Almonds and Cinnamon Drops

from the Diamond girls, Miss Ruby and Miss Pearl,
who'd savour for the coming year the boiled
demerara of their names on his tongue.

And so it was for years. He'd come from his lodgings
in the east, arriving at the Sanctus
and the priest's prayer

Hosanna in Excelsis and the women beating their breasts
mumbling *Amen* – until one year came
without his coming.

And when they swept away the crumbs
and put the sweets back in the jars
they gathered in their twos

and threes, knees crossed, drinking endless mugs
of tea, reading leaves, recalling how failed
his face had been last time

whispering he'd been overheard complain, but only once,
and even then by someone never named,
how much the Sunlight and the Cherry Blossom weighed.

Advent in Cornamona

The fold of sacking over his back
is barely able to keep the worst of the weather
out of his bones as he makes his way home
across the causeway that straddles the bog.

His wife listens for his return – soles being scraped,
the rubbing of moleskin against itself – she has spread
last Sunday's paper on the floor for him
to turn the earth out of his trouser bottoms.

Propped in front of the clock there's a letter from Mary
saying because of the baby
she'll not be making the journey
from London this Christmas after all.

They'll say nothing to one another about the letter,
but when they go to bed they'll settle into one another's shape
as boulders in one of his dry stone walls slip
one against the other shouldering a knuckle of stars.

Winter Solstice

On this the shortest day of the year unspoken with promise, I wait
by the mouth of the river beside a wood of holly

and hazel, of dwarf oak and alder, listening for the screech of snow-
geese wintering in the estuary,

keeping watch below the shallow flight of migrants for the Island
of the Moon to surface on the water

face down, its drowned tongue undertowing wind and current.
On this the longest night of the year.

And you come with dumb sound over soft ground carrying
on your feet seeds from the wood,

your arms cradling broken antlers of holly clotted
with its ooze

of berry, dressing my bare lips with the worn
velvet of your mouth,

your heel prints an archipelago of moons waning
to the crescent outline of hooves.

Ephemerella Ignita

I watched you tie
a blue-winged dun

winding on the body's bulk of fur about the hook
with loops of sooty olive silk

overshooting the shank at the gape end with wisps
of feather wetted between your lips

marvelling how you roused the warm-brown hackle of a thrush
to dress behind the eye with wings – and believed us

equal to the flight
of blue-winged flies

the pressing down of mating pairs
loading an oar with drag

equal to those short-lived on the wing
leaning into one another's eyes

on water bare as bone.

At the Eleventh Hour

Later you will come barefoot into our room to tell me there are skylarks in
the blackberry hedge masquerading as blackberry thieves. You will say they
cannot sing above the warp and woof of the thorns. I will see your tongue is
stained purple with eating the berries and will wonder how it feels for the
soul entering another life, finding its place behind the heart, growing wings.
And later while you sleep beside me in the bed we have shared for years, my
head will be bursting with mute songbirds and beggared briars.

But there's still an hour before midnight
and I'm warming your side of the bed
– a book of poems face down
on my breast – listening to you
on the flight of stairs up to the attic.
And then silence.

You have come to the broken skylight with the twisted frame that lets in the
dark. You must be wondering what to do about the stars. And listening.
Listening, for some alarm only you can hear above the rough breathing of
the poems lying on my heart.

Mayday

Here by the window
the last of the daylight falls on my page.
So far I've put nothing down on paper and the smell
of the bluebells in your mother's blue and white delph vase
is making me sleepy.

Across the room
you sprawl on my sister's old couch,
a recent copy of *Trout and Salmon* on your knee.
You're wearing your half-moon glasses on your head
and your eyes are closing.

I get up and go into the garden

– my mother's purple lilac is heady
with blossom, your grandmother's wine-red peony
will come soon, all of a rush. In June we'll have a riot
of peach-pink cupids on the rose arch you made summers ago.
In the garden next door a female blackbird flies out of a weeping ash.

There's music coming
from our daughter's bedroom.
She has left her window partly open
and the net curtain is brushing against the glass.

I go back inside

– to find a radiant-blue line of peaks
and u-shaped valleys crossing my page from left to right.
You're exactly where I left you but your eyes are open
and my pen is in the breast pocket of your shirt.

When I ask you what you've been doing
you say you've been dreaming of mayfly
swarming on an evening like this
on the far side of the lake, high above Tourmakeady.

The Kiss

Under a darkening sky they seem perfectly composed
on a bench of Liscannor slate, their bodies arranged
to cross one another in almost the letter X.

They mean this to be an important kiss – important as the first
of Diarmuid's and Grainne's year and a day of kisses
in limestone-feathered ditches

knowing, even as they kissed for the first time, Finn the great warrior
was following on the swift black mare he was given by Fiachu the farmer
who was given it by his grandfather Dil the druid.

I'm that close I can see by the way they are aligned
she cannot help but feel the buckle of his belt
in her gut. It must hurt. And how do they breath?

I cannot bear to look. Petrified I watch instead
a mute swan move with utter grace
in the mouth of the Corrib.

The Marriage Feast

And it was late in the day
when the bridegroom went to his bride
and drawing her to one side said

wife, what shall I say
such was their thirst in the day
there is no more wine. It is late,
let me send them gently away.

And his bride drawing a deep breath sighed
such dancing, such singing
they should be let dance and sing
because it is late in the day.

And her husband replied
I have not allowed for enough wine,
and besides the musicians are tired.

Then turning, his wife said
husband, do not be afraid,
let them drink from your well,
its water cool on my lips at noon
and clear enough at midnight, and still,
to hold a true outline of the moon.

They'll have no need of wine,
and we shall string dancing airs for them
on ropes you and I have twined and let down
hand over hand into the ground.

The Waiting Room

She said she was as good as dead
and sighed (as if to die
was not enough) because she'd lost her heart.

He said it was all in her head
said he wouldn't lie (nor deny
the hurt) and made her touch between her breasts

to feel its beat alert
to her open hand

– he knew best.
She'd let it go

– how was he to know
(his heart put by)

that when she touched
her breast

the beat she felt
was boast.

The Discipline Room

Perhaps she had known the cruel
extremity of ice

and looked on all things from below
with an eye that glittered

like Lucifer's. Perhaps that's why
she called it the infernal

snow and found my small
desire for it

half-witted.

All I know is this
when I was seven

snow was bliss
enough

to risk
all

– that what she did to me
had nothing

to do with justice
– that my hand

burned beneath the snow before
and after punishment.

The Recovery Room

As ash falls in upon itself, one breath
collapsed into the next

at first, then as if a *yes* and *no*
contended in her head

her breathing gained and lost
and gained

till she was strong enough
for an exercise regime.

For weeks, her breathing
done by an iron lung,

she lay in a hospital cot
runged in

the aftertaste of metal
furring her tongue

till her good lung healed
(the other one

more badly burned
had been removed)

and now the mended lung
so breathed into by iron

must lift and let fall
lift and let fall

her chest's cavity
wall

as bellows fill a rib of fire
with air.

Behind Enemy Lines

We dropped words, one step behind
our silences, expecting them to lead us
back to safe houses.

Moonstones shrouded in wild pansies,
their milky eyes waited for our return
along the same path.

Undercover of nightshade,
stepping over the silences
only one of us returned.

Whatever words not eaten
by the birds delivered themselves
darkside up

betraying whatever silences
had survived the wolves.

Sweet Afton

Flow gently Sweet Afton among thy green braes,
Flow gently I'll sing you a song in thy praise.
(Robbie Burns)

Because of the shadow on his lung
he was forbidden
to smoke

but for hours on end would sit
feeling the raised script,
humming the old air.

How are you doing today? I'd ask.
Holding on, he'd gasp,
by my finger tips.

The frogmen found him when they searched
the half-moon lake, crouched
on its bed.

He told me once, *when I was young*
I'd slit the tongues
of jackdaws

thinking it would make them sing.

Making Room

The upstairs room is tempting
– the books behind glass,
my own table on which to work,
all the paraphernalia of my craft
within reach and so ordered.

And everything in moods of blue.
A willow pattern jug for flowers, its rim
gone where swallows should've kissed.
In winter, the forced blue of hyacinths
intoxicating the room.

But it makes more sense for me to be in the thick
of crockery and cutlery, of stainless steel and aluminium,
of smells from the kitchen. In the thick of noisy children
bringing in dust and dirt from the street

not bothering to wipe their feet,
fighting over the last chocolate biscuit
in the biscuit tin or the best bit of fruit,
biting once into its flesh, or twice

then giving it to me, like it was a gift to bite
into their bite, curious about the writing
I'm at and anxious to know, *amn't I in it,
amn't I, and will it be dinnertime soon?*

In the thick of a man coming in and setting
the table to let me get on with things – holding back,
till the both of us are alone in bed, the music
he's been holding all day in his head –

and the two of us making room
for everyone to sit down and eat
in between the loose sheaves
of case notes and half-finished poems.

Spade Work
(G.S. d. 1980)

Put to the work its made for,
given weight and balance,
a spade will go in of itself
regardless of the soil

uncovering the delight
of wild roots, of bone,
of things meant to be buried
sliced right through.

You drilled me in this faith and not
to expect the steel to come
bright again

having sunk
its glitter
in the work

but still in your deep holding, keep
close

– the necessity of chance quiver
grass and wet-the-beds
self seeded

– the pale reburial
of broken remains
in ground allowed for

– the shy recovery
of things deliberately
hidden.

Damage

Before reaching the hide
I turned to find
you

loading yourself
with storm
damage.

Safe in the hide
you showed me
the broken

back of a fiddler crab,
an empty mermaid's
purse

and into the palm of my hand
you put the brittle case
of a heart urchin

as if I could stop it hurting your head.

And Then Again

just as I think I'm used to the numbing silence
of winter galleons dropping below
burned horizons

a warming voice carried by an off-shore breeze
upsets the winter mean, ropes me in.

Trust me, it says, *there is still the possibility of return
by earthsmoke, by windflower,*

*by entering into the orchard
where the last apple tree
has rotted out*

*to wonder at the suddenness
of midsummer-men,*

*the look-up-and-kiss-me
and the blue,*

*oh the blue
of forget-me-not*

and but for the *trust me*, as curing of pain
as my father's exhaled smoke fogging
the inner ear, I could shrug it off

remembering the dream I have befriended, of homecoming
merchantmen bearing close to shore in foul weather
believing too happily in false hurricane lamps.

Blaze

I despaired of ever taking your hand because of the scar
disfiguring its palm

cancelling out the chance lines of inheritance
with its blaze.

You'd say, *Put your hand*
in mine.

But I'd shy away, wondering
what if I should burn

like the mare you made right itself
as if on wings

the mare in its traces that slipped on the ice
outside our door

the mare you touched
with iron

pulled from the fire
with bare hand.

Until the day I left your house, my hand
tight in yours

– the day I chose for you to give me away.

Astray

The lining of his coat was all silkiness
smelling of inside pockets
of covert tenderness.

All my life I never knew him
step off the path he'd worn
to a shine till thin

with illness he seemed to lose
his way going from room
to room confused

by faces as familiar to him as his own.
I watched him like a child
watching for the moon

on moonless nights lost inside his coat
– not quick enough with silk
to turn it inside out.

Triptych
(for Kate Newmann)

fuchsia – deora Dé
a penitent wayfarer
also tears of God

in the fuchsia hedge
slipped from my father's garden
my shadow wavers

wanting to believe
in baptism by desire
in the gift outright

beyond the ninth wave
the impress of human feet
waiting the spring tide

overwintering
birds sing unheard through the glass
of the music room

impossible songs
i sing hymns under my breath
my ear misfiring

imagining just
one flawless agnus dei
its effortless grace

answering the song
overwintering outside
pleading for mercy

we believed her voice
urging sleep before the dark
overwhelmed our hearts

its brogue a rushlight
leading by unapproved roads
across the border

home and lost substance
the mother she'd never known
some false start redeemed

each holding the hem
of her trailing petticoat
blood not the issue

nor birthright but death
its invisible presence
kissing us goodnight

In Irish

between *breith* for birth
and the word for a slow death
there's phosphorescence

before *bás* for death
there is a breaking white wave
and a kindly soil

after death look for
an open-woven basket
and slow dipping oars